WAG THAT TAIL

A Trainer's Guide to a Happy Dog

MICHAEL SCHAIER

Design by Janet Sarah Allison

Written by Michael Schaier

michaels-pack.com

Illustration and Graphic Design by Sarah Allison

sarahallison.com

ISBN-10: 1466231076

ISBN-13: 978-1466231078

DEDICATED TO

Clarence and Rosie, you two are my inspiration. Clarence, my gentle giant, thank you for your kindness and loyalty. My sweet Rosie, your love of life and exuberant spirit leaves me in awe.

Thank you both for making me understand.

TABLE OF CONTENTS

CHAPTER FOUR

CHAPTER FIVE

CHAPTER SIX

CHAPTER SEVEN

CHAPTER THIRTEEN

CHAPTER ONE
Stressed dog = Crazy dog

"'My, what big teeth you have," said Little Red Riding Hood. 'All the better to eat you with, my dear,' said the Wolf." - Little Red Riding Hood

In 2009, the pet industry estimated that Americans spent $45.4 billion on their dogs' food, vet care, toys and training. In November 2010, Amazon.com listed 4,564 dog training books for sale. Advancements in and availability of veterinary medicine makes it easy and convenient to keep our dogs' bodies healthier. Over the last 30 years, off-leash parks, doggy play dates and doggy daycare centers have popped up nationwide. Yet, more and more of our dogs in the United States are suffering from behavior problems.

Insurance companies, the Center for Disease Control and the Journal of American Medicine all report that dog bites are on the rise and are considered an important source of injury.

- In 1986 an estimated 585,000 dog bites were reported that needed medical attention. By 1994 that number had risen to 800,000. (Dog and Cat Ownership, 1991-1998," JAMA)
- 50% of dog bites occur at home and 77% of the bites are to family and friends. (Insurance Information Institute)

Sadly, more and more Americans are sharing Little Red Riding Hood's interaction with a canine. Why are our dogs biting the hands that feed them? What are our dogs trying to tell us?

Based on archeological evidence, dogs have existed for approximately 25,000 years. For most of that time, dogs were part of our society as work mates and companions. Most historians agree they started out as sentries and freeloaders, hanging out near the human camps, eating our leftovers and warning us of human and animal intruders.

Humans, recognizing that the dogs' senses and instincts surpassed their own, started relying on the various skills of their canine companions. The dogs that were expert hunters were used to help humans track, bring down and retrieve game. The big, strong and steady dogs were used to pull carts to market and sleds for transportation. Lonely shepherds enjoyed the company and guarding behavior of the dogs with protective instincts. Even the little guys had their place, chasing off vermin and yapping at newcomers. As time went on these traits were honed and encouraged through selective breeding until we developed distinct breeds of dogs.

These dogs had a purpose in life and a demanding job. They worked side by side with their human family; often the family's survival depended in part on the dog's help. Dogs spent the day with their humans outside in their natural environment running, jumping, digging, hunting, tracking and taking down prey. At the end of the workday, both dog and master were worn out and could relax at home and enjoy the fruit of their labor. This was the dog's life.

100% Unemployment Rate for US Canines

In the last century we have seen a change from an agricultural and rural society to one that is increasingly urban or suburban. Human jobs are at desks in office buildings, not in the forest or field. Our survival no longer depends on working side by side with our dogs. As such, our dogs have lost their jobs and their reason for getting up in the morning. They are now latchkey dogs, alone in the house all day with nowhere to go and nothing to do.

When we compare the modern dog's life to the life of his ancestors, it's clear that our animals today do not get a fair opportunity to use their skills and burn off their energy. Their physical and emotional stores of energy get pent up only to be released in ways that humans deem inappropriate: barking, biting, chasing, chewing, etc. Our dogs are like time bombs waiting to go off.

**They are bored, frustrated, stressed out,
over stimulated and anxiety-ridden!**

If you want a happy and healthy dog, you'll give him an outlet for all this energy. It's called exercise and play…and a lot of it.

Get that tail wagging!

CHAPTER TWO
Stress-Management 101

There are two types of energy that circulate through us and make us want to move: physical energy and emotional energy. Both physical energy and emotional energy serve a purpose and need outlets. Physical energy is created from the food we eat and includes digestion and the chemical reactions in our cells, like ATP to ADP conversion. Physical energy is reflected in our body's strength like the size and strength of our muscles and our endurance. We can manage excesses of physical energy by going for a run, taking a bike ride and any other type of physical exertion. Emotional energy is generated by our surroundings and events in our lives as we process it through our thoughts, feelings, life experiences and personalities. A clear demonstration of emotional energy can be seen in any hospital waiting room; people are pacing, or sitting with bouncing legs, tapping fingers, twirling hair. They can't sit still. It is communicated in words like hope, fear, worry and excitement. This is emotional energy and this is where stress is generated. Stress is unresolved emotion.

We ask dogs to go against their nature, to swim upstream, every day. We ask that they do the opposite of what is normal to them.

Here are typical actions that we require of our dogs that go against their nature:

- Understand English
- Don't chase other dogs
- Don't chase the cat
- Don't jump on people
- Stay inside
- Stay outside
- Don't bark
- Don't chew on things

Our dogs don't get much control over their own lives: they don't eat or drink what or when they want or even get to choose when to take a potty break. They have no say over their home or environment. They don't speak our language and we don't speak theirs. The list goes on and on. Aren't dogs amazing creatures that they can and will adapt to our "crazy" way of life? Their adaptation comes with a price, though – stress.

Stress itself is a natural part of life and motivates us to learn and move forward through life. That feeling of being "stressed" is a normal healthy physical response in the body in response to an environment that feels hostile or dangerous.

Stress is an inevitable part of life for our dogs and us. Stress becomes troublesome when it is unresolved, unrelenting and it turns into a chronic problem. It can start to affect almost every biological system in the body. When under stress bodies release stress hormones. We all experience stress, so these hormones under normal levels are healthy and normal. But if regularly elevated, overtime the stress hormones start to lower the immune system making it harder to fight off disease.

Interestingly, stress also has an effect on the nervous system because as stress increases the body responds by releasing adrenaline. Increased levels of adrenaline is in part responsible for the "fight or flight" response in a dog. The dog's heart rate is elevated, breathing is more shallow and rapid, and muscular strength is increased. He is primed to chase and to bite.

A dog, given the chance, will attempt to burn off his own stress... but you may not like how he chooses to do it. Stressed out dogs often portray abnormal behaviors such as nervous marking, self-mutilation, barking, obsessive compulsive disorders, digging, escaping fences and aggression. The bottom line is that increased levels of the stress hormone and adrenaline are counter-productive to a happy relaxed dog.

How dogs naturally relieve stress

The natural way for dogs to relieve stress is to hunt and to play at hunting. Let's look at a wild dog. A wild dog sniffs and trots about smelling and looking for a prey animal like an unsuspecting rabbit. Something moves in the distance and the dog catches sight of the rabbit. The dog focuses on that animal and all the world disappears as he focuses so intently. Then the dog chases the rabbit, running hard and maybe for a rather long distance because rabbits are quick. He has a couple of misses – the bunny gets away. Stress and hunger build up in the dog motivating and energizing his hunt. He spots another rabbit and the chase ensues yet again. This time he catches the animal grabs him in his mouth with a powerful bite and, well, consumes the rabbit. Catching a rabbit is hard work: he must use his senses, his instincts and his physical power to succeed as a hunter. When he catches the rabbit he has overcome a major obstacle and experienced the sweet fulfillment of his work. The demands of the hunt have burned off his emotional energy (stress) and his physical energy. With a full belly and an empty battery, the dog can now relax.

Dogs also like to play "hunt". You've probably watched two dogs chase each other. One is taking on the role of the predator, (the one chasing), and the other is the prey.

On occasion, the predator-playing dog catches the prey-playing dog. They play bite and the prey-dog flips over on his back. He predator playing dog has taken down his prey! He wins! If the prey-dog is lucky, the dogs switch roles and he gets to play predator and win the next game.

Now that we understand how a dog naturally unloads stress we can use their nature to our advantage. We can help our dogs relax and stay healthy by building on these essential elements of a hunt.

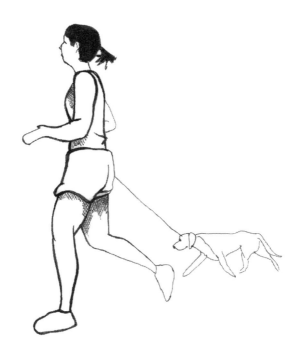

CHAPTER THREE
The Power of Intentional Excercise

As we learned in the previous chapter, exercise, and lots of it, is the key to a healthy calm pup. Turning your dog out into the backyard for a few minutes to wander around and maybe chase a few squirrels isn't the answer. Also, a slow stroll with a dog on a flexi-lead, stopping to sniff and mark mailboxes isn't the answer either. It just isn't enough to manage or burn off excess of physical or emotional energy.

Effective exercise is intentional exercise.

When I decide to work out and go for a run or a bike ride I don't stop and smell the flowers or break to chat with neighbors. I set out at specific pace for an allotted time or distance and I run or bike without stopping until I am finished.   To reap all of the benefits, exercise must be intentional and structured.

The science of fitness

Our bodies are amazingly equipped to get healthy, stay healthy, heal and adapt if given the right conditions provided by good nutrition and proper exercise. Exercise builds strength and endurance for daily life. It moderates weight. It improves health by building healthy hearts and lungs. Exercise provides joints the movement they need to stay lubricated and to keep cartilage healthy. And most importantly for behavior modification, good hard exercise produces endorphins.

Ahhh! Endorphins! Endorphins are neurotransmitters that are released in the brain during exercise. Endorphins are responsible for the feeling of the "runner's high" which is a calm sense of well being. As you exercise your dog every day you flood his brain with these feel good chemicals.

Defining trot, canter and gallop

Considering the wide variety of shapes and sizes of dogs, it's surprising that all dogs share the same patterns of movement and gaits. "Gait" is the speed and fashion in which a dog moves forward. The most common are the walk, trot, canter and gallop.

Walk

A walk is, of course, a dog's slowest speed. This is usually characterized by one foot moving forward at a time while the other three feet stay on the ground. This is usually what your dog will do inside your house.

Canter

A canter is a more off-beat sounding stride because the front legs do not move in unison, neither do the back. For small dogs, you will be able to speed walk to get your dogs up to a canter but you will likely need to jog to get the dog to speed up into a gallop. For medium dogs, you may be able to run fast enough to canter with your dog, but you'll have to get on a bike to move fast enough to get a dog into a gallop. And for you large dog owners, you will likely need a bike for both the canter and gallop.

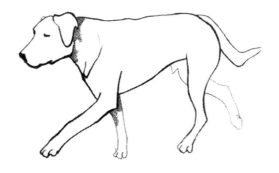

Trot

A trot is a speed walk or jog for dogs. It's the natural speed of a dog navigating in the wild. When a dog trots, like in the above picture, the dog's diagonal legs move forward together – so the dog's front left moves forward as the dog's back right leg moves forward. This is the gait used in endurance exercises; because it is a symmetrical gait both the left and right side of the dog get an even workout and build muscles on both sides. If you have a small dog you will be able to walk comfortably as your dog trots. For medium sized dogs, you will be walking at a brisk pace up to a jog. For large dogs, you will likely need to jog to get the dog to a trot speed.

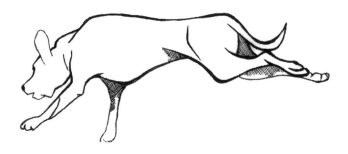

Gallop

The canter and gallop are running gaits. These are great strength building gaits – short bursts of running provides dogs with core building exercise. It's easiest to think of a gallop as the gait of racehorses – the front legs move together as one unit and the back legs move together as one unit. This is the fastest gait.

Practical guide to conditioning your dog

At this point, we are going to assume that your dog is physically healthy enough to begin a new exercise program. The first step is always to leash your dog. Even if you are going to run in a fenced park or your own acreage leash up your dog. If your dog isn't leashed you can't dictate his speed and teach him the proper work ethic: running at a speed that you dictate, beside you without stopping.

You want to move forward together with your dog safely beside you. To do this you will want to use a 6 foot or shorter leash, not a retractable leash. Leash up your dog and take him outside. If your dog gets super excited about walks and his leash, ignore it for now and let his excitement inspire you. You are going for a run!! Let him bound and bounce around for a few minutes on his leash to burn off the edge of his energy and then give him a few minutes to wander around to potty. A few minutes of slow movement is a good warm up before exercise.

Gather your dog on the side of you that you prefer; the left side is the traditional position for a heel but if you are more comfortable with your dog on the right that is okay. What is important is that you pick a side and consistently keep your dog there. Use a verbal cue to alert Rover to your intention to move, "Rover, let's go!" And start walking or jogging.

The most comfortable and efficient speed for a dog over a long distance is a trot. Get your dog up to a trot speed and maintain it without stopping. If your dog tends to pull on his leash you may find that this problem self-corrects if you will pick up your pace a little. Most dogs can maintain a trot at a fairly rapid speed.

30 days to a strong healthy body

Your dog can reach a fit body condition in as little as a 30 days. There are three elements to every conditioning program: intensity, duration and frequency. This is a very physically conservative introductory schedule to running your dog. We start very slowly with the duration and intensity. However, YOU are the expert on your dog. You can determine if your dog needs to progress more slowly or if your dog can handle a quicker ramp up time. But if you are both novices to exercise, this is a good place to start to minimize soreness and stiffness – yours and the dogs!

Here is how this schedule breaks down:

Days 1 – 5	15 minutes
Day 6	18 minutes
Day 7	Rest or a slow easy stroll
Days 8 - 11	18 minutes
Days 12 – 13	21 minutes
Day 14	Rest or a slow easy stroll
Days 15 – 17	21 minutes
Days 18 – 20	24 minutes
Day 21	Rest or a slow easy stroll
Days 21 & 22	24 minutes
Days 23 – 27	27 minutes
Day 28	Rest or a slow easy stroll
Days 29 – forever	30 minutes!
	You've made it!

Start at a 15 minute trot, morning and evening, and add three minutes to the duration every 5 days. Rest is a critical factor in any exercise program. Set aside one day for rest out of every 7 days of exercise. Depending on the dog, he may want to sleep and hang out on his rest day or he may enjoy a quiet stroll.

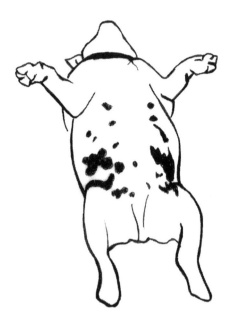

Do not be surprised if your dog acts tired and doesn't do much playing or running around the first day or two after the duration has been increased. The goal is to have a happily relaxed dog that enjoys his daily runs with you. As his owner, you and only you can determine if your dog is doing too much or too little.

For some breeds, like toy breeds, and for some senior dogs two 30 minute trots every day is all the exercise they need and want. But if you have a young sporting, working or protection breed dog, like Cocker Spaniels, Labradors or Germans Shepherds, two 30 minutes runs per day is barely challenging their physical abilities.

Depending on the dog's inherited drive and his own personality, he may enjoy more activity.

You will know if your dog is getting enough exercise by watching what he does during the day after his morning run. If he goes to bed and sleeps through the day he is getting enough. If he is up and wandering around the house barking at neighbors and looking for something to do the dog needs more exercise. A healthy adult dog sleeps about 18 hours a day – if your dog isn't sleeping during the day it is because his emotional and physical energy reserves are still full.

Once your dog is in good physical condition and has adapted to the workouts you can switch up the workouts to better fit into your own schedule while maintaining your dog's fitness and exercise needs.

For example, Mondays, Wednesdays and Fridays can be endurance days. On these days the dog works harder and longer. You can continue with 2 x 20-30 minute trots and even add a weighted backpack if your dog needs to work harder. (For more information on backpacks see Chapter Ten). Follow the trot with a 5 or 10 minute of sessions of proprioception work followed by a few minutes of gentle stretches. Or you could do a quick 10 minute trot warm up followed by 10 minutes of water retrieves or fetch. Tuesdays, Thursdays and Saturdays are lighter days where you take the dog for a trot for 10 or 15 minutes in the morning or evening followed by 5 minutes of proprioceptive work. You and the dog get Sundays off.

Air Rover

Last time I checked, Nike isn't making impact absorbing running shoes for dogs – yet. Until there is an Air Rover that will lessen the impact of running on joints, aim to run on softer surfaces when you can. Stating the obvious, there are bio-mechanical differences between our dogs and us. When we run, all of our weight is borne on our legs

and lower back. However, our dogs have the advantage of having four feet on the ground and so they can disperse their weight and the impact of running more widely across joints. However, the impact still exists. The goal is not to eliminate all impact because a moderate amount is required to build bone density, but to keep it moderate.

There's no ideal surface to run on as there are advantages and disadvantages to all of them. The healthiest route is to include a variety to your workout. Grass, dirt and mulch are the best low impact option. If your dog has a history of joint disease then you should run a majority of the time on these soft surfaces. The disadvantage to these surfaces is that unless you are running on manicured turf, like football fields or golf courses, you will need to keep a watchful eye for hidden holes or other hazards like covered rocks or slippery patches.

Asphalt is another good option; it is usually a smooth reliable surface and it is 10 times softer to run on than concrete. The danger of asphalt is that it can get dangerously hot in the summer burning exposed paw pads and the roughness of the surface can also wear on paw pads. Concrete is a widely used material and generally what sidewalks are. The hardness of concrete causes the most stress to bones, joints, ligaments and tendons. However, it stays cooler than asphalt in the summer. It is also rough on paw pads over time.

If you live near a beach, you can try some sand running to really give your dogs legs and stabilizing muscles a work-out. The best option is to mix it up – variety in running surfaces will challenge muscle memory and keep your workouts with your dog interesting. And don't forget to run hills and stairs because they will give your dog Buns of Steel!

Poop happens.

He who leaves dog poop behind will be the first
to step in it.

Of course you always carry a poop bag with you when
you are out with your dog. You don't want to have
bad poop karma, do you?

Regular exercise gets the bowels moving so don't be
surprised if the first few days of the program your dog
relieves himself multiple times. Just remember to bring
extra bags! In the long run your dog will learn to time
his need to poop around his running schedule and that's
great! It means that when you leave for work in the morning
after your run you will know for sure that your dog has
already done his business for the day and when you
go to bed at night after your evening run you won't
have to worry about the need for a 2 AM potty break.

Also, poop is a good indicator of your dog's health. Lucky
you, as you pick up your dog's poop every day you will
get to monitor your dog's digestive health. You will notice
if it is it formed or loose, odd looking or smelling, or full of
undigested material or fur. Do you see worms? Are there
chewed up pieces of your child's missing toy? Has your
dog not gone at all? Your veterinarian will thank you for
being such a responsible monitor of your dog's health and
your fellow citizens will thank you for scooping the poop.

Interval Training

Once you and your dog are up to top condition you may learn to love your new fitness regime. I know your dog will! Here are some suggestions for adding variety to your work out to keep your brain and muscles challenged.

One way to keep things interesting is to introduce intervals. Interval training combines different activities with variables in intensity and duration. The duration of the training depends on the intensity of the activity; if you increase the intensity you should decrease the duration and build up slowly over time. An intervals workout is very challenging and tiring. In this case, more is not better. You should limit interval-training sessions to one per week.

Here are a few examples of interval workouts:

10-15 min warm up trot	5 min canter	5 min trot	5 min canter	5 min cool down walk and stretch
15 min warm up trot	2 min gallop	10 min trot	3 min gallop	5 min cool down trot and stretches
7 min swim	10 min trot with backpack	10 min proprioception exercise	5 minutes stretches	
5 min swim	5 min trot with backpack	5 x50 yard fetches	5 min cool down walk	

Please remember that our goal with intentional exercise is exertion, not exhaustion. Working your dog to exhaustion every day can lead to illness and injury. Dogs on both ends of the age range, puppies and seniors, are especially prone to overdoing it. Keep an eye on your dog for signs of physical exhaustion such as dragging behind in exercise, lethargy and irritability.

Also, it is important to avoid falling into the weekend warrior syndrome where you and your dogs lay around all week and then workout hard on the weekends. This, too, can quickly lead to injuries and orthopedic problems.

What I have laid out here is an ideal. In the perfect world you would be able to trot your dog on your left without stopping and without distractions, running on a soft surface with some variety in your workouts with your dog for 30 minutes twice a day. However, do not let the ideal get in the way of starting a new habit and sticking with it. If you can't find a soft surface immediately, run anyway. If you must miss a workout, don't let it stop you from doing the next one.

Don't let missing one element of the ideal prevent you from starting a healthy new routine.

CHAPTER FOUR
It just ain't gonna happen

Do you fit one of these scenarios?

- You are afflicted with the deadly couch potato virus, a laziness-causing disease
- You are a senior citizen who has difficulty walking your dog
- You have physical disabilities that affect your mobility
- You live in a climate with winter or summer weather extremes that makes it unpleasant to be outside

You know your dog needs the exercise… but going for a run just isn't going to happen. Either you can't do it, or you just won't. What can you do?

There are lots of options to explore if running your dog every day isn't a possibility for you. You can invest in a treadmill or borrow a friend's treadmill. Look for a doggy gym nearby with treadmills. You can hire a dog walker. Or even better, ask a neighborhood high school kid who runs every day if he would take your dog with him. The raciest option is to buy a helmet and learn to "jor" with your dog.

The Treadmill is your friend

Bella the Weimaraner belongs to a busy family of four. She, like most Weimaraner, is full of energy and loves to run. Her yard is very small and her owners just don't have the time or energy at the end of the day after work and chasing young children to run Bella as much as she wants or needs. So, they bought her a treadmill.

Bella took to the treadmill instantly without any reservation. Frequently her owners will find her standing on the treadmill patiently waiting for someone to turn it on! They often joke about how Bella loves it so much she wishes they would put her on the treadmill before they leave for work and leave it running so she could run all day long.

Dogs love to run. Don't be surprised if your dog takes to the treadmill quickly – and asks for more. The beauty of a treadmill is that you stand still or possibly even sit while your dog runs which makes this a great option for people who are physically unable (or unwilling) to adequately exercise a dog.

The treadmill may also be the answer for people who have dogs with certain behavioral problems that make it difficult to handle the dog outside. Some dogs, from sheer exuberance and strength, could harm the people on the other side of their leash. And some dogs are not yet ready for their public debut due to dog aggression, human aggression, cat or car chasing, or other safety issues. Yet it is critically important that dogs with such behaviors get lots and lots of exercise. Over time, a stringent exercise program on a treadmill may ameliorate or soften a dog's reactivity so that outdoor activities can be reintroduced. Certainly, the dog's reactivity levels will drop enough for the owners to start working with their dog, with a trainer, to solve the dog's particular triggers.

Guide to safely working out on a treadmill

Treadmills come in varied sizes, but most dogs will fit safely on most average sized treadmills. If you have a bigger or leggy dog, you need to make sure that the platform and belt (the running surface) is long and wide enough for a full length gait.

The location of the treadmill in the room is important. You will want one of the long sides of the treadmill pushed up against a wall. The wall acts as a guard to keep your dog safely on the belt and to prevent him from trying to jump off that side. It is also important that the front of the treadmill not face a wall but out into a room or hall. If the dog is running on the treadmill toward a wall he may actually fear running into the wall. This, too, can cause a dog to shorten or stilt his gait.

Before you put your dog on a treadmill, take him out to pee and poop first. Running gets the bowels moving, so you really will want to ensure that your dog is empty before you begin a workout.

To introduce your dog to the treadmill, leash him up with a 6-foot leash and ask the dog to step up onto the center of the belt. Hold the leash tightly from the front of the treadmill and start the belt moving at a very slow pace. Remember praise and encouragement will go a long way. Hold on tightly enough to keep the dog centered while the dog acclimates to the movement. If for some reason this position is difficult for you, you may try standing on the other long side of the treadmill and face the same direction of the dog actually straddling your dog. Put your foot on the edge of the treadmill, but not the part that is moving. Use your arms to hold the dog's leash centered on the belt.

Do not tie the dog to the treadmill at any point. Do not leave the dog unattended while the belt is moving. This is a huge safety hazard.

While in the learning stages keep distractions to a minimum so that the dog focuses on moving forward, not turning around or looking around and accidentally stepping off the side. Start with a short session and end it while the dog is having fun. Most dogs acclimate readily to running on the treadmill. When your dog is comfortable, slowly increase the speed up to a trot. From there you can progress to any speed or incline that your treadmill offers.

Options for the Lazy (you know who you are…)

Use a treadmill – the dog runs and you sit.

Ask a friend who is runner to take your dog while you make lemonade.

Hire someone to run your dog while you sleep.

Find a hill and play fetch uphill.

Ask a trainer to teach your dog how to perform the strength exercises and then do them at home, sitting in your recliner.

Put on roller skates and harness dog power.

As you float around your pool invite your dog in with you and drop treats in the water for him to swim around to get.

Hire a dog walker

There are people who walk and run dogs for a living. They are experts at exercising a dog and they will come to your house – no need to go anywhere! The downside is that you will have to pay for the service. You may have to pay extra to get a private walk or to get an intentional non-stop exercise trot. But in return you get a calm healthy tired dog.

Another option is to recruit a neighborhood high school kid who is responsible and runs regularly to train for a sport. Many high schools have a volunteerism requirement to graduate, so if you are disabled or a senior citizen you could call your local high school's track and field coach and ask if any of his runners would volunteer to exercise your dog a few days a week.

"Joring"

The coolest option is to learn to "jor" with your dog. Joring refers to any type of dog-powered activity. Joring feeds off dogs' natural desire to run and pull. The concept is that the dog is fitted in a harness and hooked to a long lead. The lead is connected to a mode of transportation – a cart, bike, scooter, wheelchair, etc. The dog, or dogs, pulls from the front like dog sledding while his person rides.

The joring sport community states that ANY dog can pull a scooter or a wheelchair. Even the little ones. Joring allows you get to participate in your dog's exercise and get outside with them. The downside, and it is small, is that there is a little bit of training and skill involved but not so much that you couldn't learn to do it alone. You'll need to buy a harness for the dog and a cart, bike scooter, wheelchair, skates, or some other mode of transportation for you. Oh, and a helmet.

There are heaps of online resources to help you get started. Dogscooter.com is a great place to start with demonstrations of dogs pulling, training resources, and   contact   numbers   for   area   joring   clubs.

Perhaps the idea of dog-power doesn't suit you, you could always let your dog run beside you as you tool around a park in your wheelchair, on a bike or even on roller blades.

CHAPTER FIVE
Recovering your Playful Nature

Come on, confess! When was the last time you played with your dog? I mean really played hard with him. You picked up a plush squeaky toy, wagged it around in your dog's face and then took off running, toy in hand, inviting a rigorous game of chase with your dog. After 5 minutes of running circles around your yard, occasionally stopping short and showing off your best spin moves, your dog catches you as you both crash breathlessly happy to the grass and lie there together watching the clouds. Sounds lovely, doesn't it?

Why don't we do play with our dogs like that more often? Where is our spontaneity? Our playfulness? Our dogs are not a necessary part of our existence anymore... so if they aren't our playmates then what is the point? Humans and dogs alike love games. And who among us couldn't use a little more fun in our lives? We get so busy these days and work so hard that sometimes even our play and leisure activities become serious and work-like. Let your dog inspire you to let your playful side out. Who cares if your neighbors talk about you... they probably do anyway.

Intentional exercise helps us manage stress and takes the edge off of our physical energy reserves and playtime helps us relieve our emotional energy stores and helps us to relax. Play is about joy and pleasure and feeling like young again. Play time also provides mental conditioning; fun games teach us focus, restraint, trust and teamwork. The same is true for our dogs. Dogs who are given the opportunity to play hard learn to tolerate greater levels of stress without any negative consequences.

Compare the release a dog gets from "the hunt" to the stress release we humans get from playing a sport, like racquetball, for fun. You focus intently on the ball. You run and swing at the ball. Hopefully, you get to enjoy the feeling of making contact with the ball. Your brain keeps you focused on following the rules of the game. It requires coordination and is physically demanding.

The instincts you have developed over the months or years you've played racquetball guide your body's movements as you move around the court. It's fun and it feels good whether you win or lose. But of course, it's more fun and more satisfying to win.

Chase

You're it! In the game of chase "it" is the one who is being chased. The game is simple: you grab a handful of treats or your dog's favorite toy and head outside. You show your dog the loot, waggling it in front of him to get him jacked up for a game and then you take off running! You zig! You zag! You circle back! And your dog runs after you chasing you. After a few minutes or when you get winded, you let the dog catch you and you give him the loot.

When you play chase with your dog you always want to be "it". Your dog is never "it". The most evident reason is that we don't want our dogs to learn to run away from us or that we are willing to chase them. Here's why; imagine you and Rover are at the park. Rover finds a dead squirrel

and is carrying it around in his mouth. Not good. You run toward your dog to get him to drop the squirrel but your dog runs away. It's a game! To him. He's declared himself "it". For you, it's a game of ultimate frustration because dogs are nimble and fast and you'll never catch him. We don't want to teach our dogs that running away from us is the right thing to do or the fun thing to do. We want our dogs to want to run to us and we want to develop that habit.

Another reason why you are always "it" and the dog is never "it" is that in his world, the object being chased is the prey, even when it is just a game. We humans are bigger and stronger than most dogs and we also control their whole world, so being chased by a human can easily frighten a dog. Human-as-predator and dog-as-prey is a model we want to avoid with our dogs. We humans have an innate understanding of this fear. Do you remember back when you were a small child being chased by your dad or big brother? You knew that it was just a game but after a few minutes of it you got scared! They were bigger than you were and stronger than you so being chased wasn't fun! We want our dogs to be magnetized to us not scared of us.

By being "it" you also get to control the starting and ending of the game, along with the intensity. It is not the intent of the game to tease the dog into a frenzy or get the him over-stimulated. If you sense that your dog is starting to get carried away then let him "catch" you and end the game by giving him the loot. You can calm your dog with a nice massage in the grass, teaching him to relax after game time.

Playing chase satisfies a few elements of a play hunt. It teaches them that we humans are fun not scary and to running toward us is fun! And at the end of their play hunt, they get the loot – their favorite toy or the treats! That's a very satisfying game for a dog. Why would he want to chase a squirrel or the UPS man if he gets to catch you? He'll never catch the squirrel or the UPS truck (or we hope not!) but he can catch you!

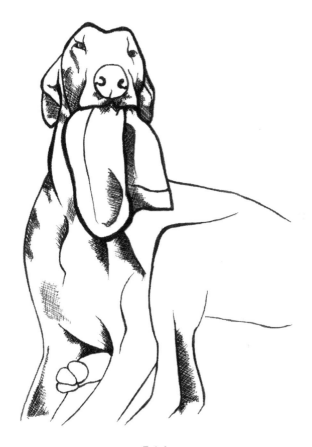

Fetch

If you have a working or sporting breed dog then your dog has probably already taught you that dogs love to play fetch. But even if you have a non-sporty dog, he can learn to fetch because once the drive to chase and catch is triggered all dogs love to do it. And this is a great game for you because you get to stand still while your dog does all the running.

The first step, as always, is to leash up and go outside. If you go to a park, you may need a long lead, 50 to 100 feet, to give your dog the freedom to really run and still meet the local leash law requirements. The game is simple – you throw something and the dog runs to get it and bring it back to you. You throw it again. And again. And again.

Many dogs do some wild acrobatics when they play fetch - jumping in the air, twisting into back flips and stopping short trying to catch the ball before it lands. It's fun to watch our dogs do these acrobatic feats, but it isn't particularly safe. The jumping, twisting and flipping can lead to muscle and ligament tears and back problems. Awkward landings can wrench knees and elbows. You really do want to avoid having your dog land on his back legs – they are not designed for that movement and can easily be injured.

To practice safe fetching you want to throw the ball or toy far enough so that it lands on the ground and stops rolling before your dog reaches the reaches it. Also, to prevent your dog from jumping up in the air try to throw it really high or very low to the ground.

If you have a big fast dog, getting enough distance on the ball can be difficult but there are ball launchers, like the Chuck-It, that can add several yards to your throw.

So what do you do if your dog won't give you the toy for you to throw it again? Well, you can ask your trainer to help teach your dog to "Drop". But, for the sake of the game, play with 2 identical toys. Your dog will want the toy that you have in your hand more than the one in his mouth, especially if you are enticing him with it. He will drop the one in his mouth and go after the one you are offering. When you have had enough of playtime, simply offer your dog a treat and pick up both toys and head inside to relax.

If you have access to a pool or lake you can add a whole new element to fetch by throwing the ball or a floating toy into the water and letting your dog swim for it. This is a great way to exercise in the summer heat!

Tug of War

Dogs love this game. Dogs need to play this game. Of all the games you can play with your dog, 'Tug of War' is the most likely to satisfy his hunting drive and provide a great deal of stress relief. While playing tug, dogs get to bite, and bite hard, and yank like crazy as if they are bringing down prey. The dog gets to be a DOG with you. How exciting! This game is most fun when it is intense so it is probably not a game for your children to play with the dog, and never unsupervised.

Here's how the game is played. You leash up your dog and head outside. On your way out, pick up a long plush squeaky toy or a rope toy and tease your dog with it. He grabs one end and you grab the other. You tug and the dog tugs back. You get tired and you let the dog win by dropping your end. Woohoo! He gets the prey!

Remember, this is a game and the dog knows it is just a game, too. Beating your dog at Tug of War to gain his respect is like beating your 5 year old nephew at basketball so that he learns to respect you... winning is not terribly satisfying for you and it is discouraging for him. This isn't about who is bigger, stronger and in control. It's a fun game. Your dog wins the games but YOU control when you play it and for how long. You initiate and end the game.

If you start to see that your dog gets over stimulated or frenzied, simply drop your end and let him win. If you haven't played much tug with your dog he may need to build both the physical and emotional channels to play for longer periods of time without getting out of sorts. To help your dog stay grounded you want to keep your tugs long and smooth – no short yanks and no shaking or pulling hard enough for your dog's feet to come off the ground. The dog might initially play growl and shake his end, and if so just pick up the leash and jog around the yard letting your dog work out

some energy by carrying the toy around in his mouth.

If your dog has been harshly corrected for using his mouth or for chewing and nipping as a puppy he may be a little reluctant to play tug. Don't give up! If your dog loves tennis balls, tie a tennis ball in an old sock and tug with that until he gets used to the game.

Reluctant dogs or dogs who need to do more running may really enjoy Fetch-Tug or Chase-Tug, or the ultimate Chase-Fetch-Tug game. For Fetch-Tug, find a tug toy that has some weight so that it can be thrown. Throw the toy and let the dog fetch it back to you and then

play tug with him. In Chase-Tug, you play the game of chase but instead of giving him the toy at the end of the chase you only offer him one end, let him bite it and play tug and then drop your end and let him win. For a really physically challenging game, play Chase-Fetch-Tug; play Chase and then when the dog catches you throw the toy for him to fetch. When he brings it back to you, you grab one end and tug with him.

Hide and Seek

This game doesn't require explanation, does it? If you have a secured yard you go hide and your dog runs to find you. Repeat. If your dog doesn't notice that you're missing when you run off to hide, well, then, you've got a problem! Try feeding your dogs a few treats or playing a quick game of chase to put you on Rover's radar and alert him that it is playtime.

You can amplify the excitement of 'Hide and Seek' by taking your dog and a friend with you to a park. You run and hide while your friend holds the dog's leash. When you've hidden, your friend encourages your dog to seek you out. As your dog learns the game you can find more difficult hiding places or move further away. If your dog is a scenting breed, like a hound or a spaniel, you'll really enjoy watching them use their natural ability to sniff you out.

To really boost the mental workout, you could put your dog in a sit/stay or down/stay while you go hide and then call once for him to come. You can make it even harder by putting him in a stay position with his back turned toward you as you run to hide.

Playing 'Hide and Seek' is great tool for magnetizing your dog to you. It teaches your dog to look for you and keep an eye on you. It's your dog's job to stay with you, not the other way around. Playing a few rounds of 'Hide and Seek' is a great warm up exercise before you start off-leash work or you are start on an off leash hike.

Remember, playing with your dog lays the foundation for a strong relationship with your dog built on reciprocal trust.   In the end, owner-dog trust is the key to having a balanced dog.

CHAPTER SIX
Safety, Strength, and Stretching

Young or old and regardless of breed, a dog needs exercise just like we humans do to maintain a happy healthy body. If your dog hasn't been to the vet in a year or more or if you are unsure about the health of your dog, the vet must be your first step. A trustworthy veterinarian will give your dog a thorough exam, including asking you about your dog's current activities, lifestyle and diet. Tell your vet that you would like to start an exercise program with your dog and you would like to know of any pre-existing medical conditions that would affect how you and your dog exercise.

Here is some information you may
want to glean from the exam:

- Is my dog's weight ideal for his size and breed?
- What is the exercise tolerance for my dog's breed?
- Is my dog healthy enough to begin an exercise program?
- Do you consider my dog a puppy, an adult or a senior?
- If my dog is a senior, are his joints and heart healthy?
- At this stage, what is a safe level of activity for my dog?

If you veterinarian does discover some sort of physical condition, like hip dysplasia or osteoarthritis or a heart murmur he will be able to recommend a specialist and a suitable exercise routine for you. It isn't the end of the road for your dog, in fact, it just may be the beginning of a healthy new road. Ask your veterinarian to consult with or refer you to a specialist, like a rehabilitation and conditioning veterinarian. These vets are skilled at identifying and correcting nervous and mobility issues and can tailor make a program specifically for your dog.

Just like with humans, there are four areas of exercise that we must pay attention to in order to have a balanced fitness program for a dog:

1. endurance
2. proprioception
3. strength
4. flexibility

The first area of exercise, endurance, is covered by the intentional running program in Chapter Two. You will be amazed at how quickly your dog builds muscle tone simply from going on a few quick jogs every day.

Proprioception

The second type of exercise is called proprioception. Proprioception is the sense of knowing where each body part is in space without looking. This is a learned skilled. A human example is learning ballroom dance steps without having to watch your feet. Eventually, with practice, you know where your feet are without looking down.

Proprioception exercises strengthen the communication between the nervous system and the muscles. These exercises are important to practice and important

in daily life for safety reasons; it is the key to good balance and coordination.

Strength

The third type of exercise is strength training. This is the area most overlooked by dog owners. Strong muscles are vital to living a healthy life because they make daily tasks easier by preventing fatigue. Also, big strong muscles burn more calories and guard against injury and help to keep joints stable and healthy. These specific muscle building exercises will help keep them strong and buff. See the following chart for fun strength training and proprioception exercises.

74

Exercise	Effect	Repetitions
Dog Squats Have dog sit making sure he sits squarely on both haunches. Ask him to stand.	Strengthens legs and hips	Start with 3 repetitions. Gradually build up to 30 to 50 reps. As dog gets stronger squats can be add mid- or post run.
Sitting Pretty Put dog in a sit. Use treats to lure the dog to sit up into a "beg" stance. This requires some learned skill so as the dog is learning position his back to a couch or wall so he won't fall backwards.	Core muscles and neck.	
Advanced: As the dog gets stronger and more skilled add to the challenge by encouraging the dog to continue from the begging position to standing on his hind limbs and back down.	Adds leg and hip strength.	
Figure 8's Begin by walking your dog in a wide 20 ft long figure 8 pattern. As the dog gets accustomed to this exercise reduce and tighten the size of the Figure 8. Advanced: Increase the speed of the dog's gait on both curves of the Figure 8	Proprioception and range of motion in the hips and spine	5 or 6 repetitions
Side Sit-ups Position dog to lying on his side. Use a treat to draw up the dog's head by slowly tracing a line along his spine to his hip and knee and back down again.	Core muscles	5 reps on each side
Ladder Steps Place a ladder flat on the ground. With a leash on, very very slowly walk the dog through the ladder rungs. You want him to think about where each foot is being placed so move slowly. The goal is for him to put his foot on the ground, not on the rung or outside of the ladder. Advanced: Using treats, have the dog walk backward through the ladder rungs.	Proprioception	Unlimited repetitions

Stretching

Stretching is simply the flexion and extension of limbs, muscles and joints. Stretching exercises improve flexibility and range of motion in joints – they also feel really good and are quite relaxing. Stretching exercises are also a great way to bond with your dog, helping him learn to relax and it gives you a good opportunity to examine his body from nose to tail on a regular basis.

There are two types of stretching exercises: passive and active. Passive stretching is stationery and should feel like cuddle time to the dog. It is very important to note that cold muscles should not be stretched. These exercises are for after a workout or a warm up session. Find a quiet environment where there are few distractions. Get your dog to lie down and spend some time petting him until he is relaxed.

Passive Stretching

The goal of passive stretching is for each muscle to be lengthened and strengthened. Each joint should be exercised separately. Using a soft touch, start gently and gradually lengthen each limb, slowly increasing the pressure to what the dog will accept comfortably. Don't pull or push the limbs when stretching, but guide the leg into the stretch until you feel light resistance. If your dog is uncomfortable he will pull his leg back and you don't want to go that far. Do not twist the joints.

Gently massage the muscles you are stretching. These stretches should never ever hurt! Each stretch should be held for approximately 10-15 seconds. Unlike knee and elbow joints, the hip and shoulder joints rotate so they can be moved in circles starting with small rotation and gradually over time (days or weeks) increase the range of motion. The emphasis here is to be gentle and gradual.

Active Stretching

Active stretching serves as both a stretch and a good warm up before a workout. These still require a gentle touch and small movements as the dog's body is introduced to new ways of moving. See the chart below for fun strength exercises.

Stretch	Effect	Repetitions
Leg weaving Stand with your feet greater than hip width apart. With a leash or a treat guide your dog to weave in and out in tight circles between your legs.	Stretches the spine, the sides and hips.	10 repetitions
Stand tall Ask dog to "hup" by putting his front paws up on you. You gently pull and stretch your dog's body straight up.	Full body stretch	3 reps
Dog C Place dog in a standing position and use a treat to slowly draw his head and neck to	Flexes and stretches the spine.	10 repetitions to each location

CHAPTER SEVEN
The Hourglass Figure: Canine Obesity

There is no breed standard which states that the ideal dog of that breed should be "flabby, moderately overweight and with a pendulous abdomen!"

Steven B. Fox, DVM, info@cva.com

Canine obesity is an epidemic. Like most American humans, most American dogs are overfed and under-exercised. Unless your veterinarian cries out in delight at your dog's weight and physical condition, it is safe to assume your canine pal could stand to lose a few pounds.

Don't take it personally!

To the modern American eye, a dog carrying extra pounds looks healthy and normal. Canine athlete veterinarian, Dr. Fox conservatively estimates that 50% of the competitive dog athletes he examines are overweight and 25% of them are obese! These dogs aren't just pets – they are the cream of the crop in their sports and even still their weight is too high. We Americans just tend to like the look of pudgy dogs, but that doesn't make it right or safe.

So what if your dog is a little pudgy? What's the big deal if your dog is carrying just a few extra pounds? Just like with humans, obesity puts dogs at risk for a variety of health problems.

A dog at his ideal weight has 16-25% body fat. An overweight dog is 26-35% body fat and a dog who is considered obese has 35%+ body fat. Labrador Retrievers are one of the breeds of dog that can easily accumulate extra weight. According to the American Kennel Club, a male Labrador Retriever in working condition (top physical shape) that is 24 ½ inches tall at the shoulders (top of the range for height for a male Lab) should weigh no more than 80 lbs. This dog is at his ideal weight for his height at 80 lbs has 16-20 lbs of body fat. Let's say that the dogs gains 20 lbs and is now obese.

Every pound of fat contains a mile of capillaries.

The heart has to pump enough blood to carry nutrients through all of those new extra capillaries. This poor Lab, who now weighs 100 lbs., has 20 miles of extra capillaries – 20 miles!   This adds a lot of unneeded stress on his poor heart. But it isn't just the heart that suffers – his lungs do too as the dog tries to carry the extra weight and get enough oxygen to all of his cells. Excess weight can cause respiratory problems in hot weather and makes it more difficult for the dog to exercise. And just like with humans, obesity can lead to diseases like diabetes, cancer and joint disease. This leads to high veterinary bills for you and a shortened life span for your dog.

How to determine if your dog is overweight

Dr. Fox recommends the following three steps to determine if your dog is at his best weight:

> 1.   "Check the neck: press your thumb and index finger deep into the side of the neck just ahead of the shoulder, and pinch them together. If your fingers are more than 1/2" apart, the dog is overweight. (Note: this is where old dogs tend to carry most of their excess fat, and they

may actually be thin in other locations.)

2. "Check the ribs: stand with your dog beside you facing his butt. Place your thumb on the middle of his spine half way down the back and spread your fingers out over his last few ribs. Then run your fingers up and down along his skin. You should be able to feel the bumps of his ribs without pressing in."

3. "Check the hips: run your hand over your dog's croup (top of the dog's butt between the loin and the tail). You should be able to feel the bumps of his two pelvic bones without pressing down."

For a visual representation of what a normal, overweight and obese dogs looks like see the Body Condition Scale below.

Canine Body Condition Scale

| Healthy | Overweight | Obese |

In the healthy weighted dog, notice that from above the waist is visible and the dog has an hourglass form. In the side view, there is a noticeable tuck separating the chest from the hind end. The ribs are right below the skin and easily palpable. (Squeezing fat to find ribs doesn't count.)

The cause of obesity in an otherwise healthy animal is simple: too many calories and not enough exercise. Unless you have taught your dog how to open your refrigerator, he is only eating what you give him to eat. While a dog's natural energy level varies with age, sex, and neuter status the dog's activity level is wholly dependent on the people he spends his time with. If his family doesn't exercise, it is likely that the dog doesn't either.

Doggy Weight Loss Diet

Most dogs consume more calories than they need to support their activity levels. When it comes to feeding your dog, don't believe the bag! Most people follow the recommending feeding guidelines on their bag of kibble but for most dogs the recommended feeding is 20-30% too much food. One half to ¾ of the recommended amount of kibble from most manufacturers is more than enough for most dogs. Even the most active young dogs do not usually need the full amount of food

recommended on the bag. If your dog needs to lose a few pounds, you can start by cutting back his daily food by 30%: if he usually eats three cups, he now eats 2 cups.

It is very important to measure the food with a level measuring cup so you know exactly how much our dog is eating. If a dog is hungry he will easily finish his meal in under five minutes. Measure a certain amount of kibble and put in it your dog's bowl. Put the bowl down for your dog and give him 15 minutes to eat and then pick up the bowl. That's it. No more food until the next meal. Your dog is not going to starve to death overnight. And please, no free feeding.

This is an easy fix, right? Feed your dog less and exercise him more. But, what about those big sad hungry eyes? What do you do when he looks at his food bowl and notices that there is less, a lot less, in there? You can plump up his kibble by letting it soak in and soak up a little water before serving. Also, you can replace the "missing" 1/3 of his food with a few frozen or canned green beans (no salt added) or canned pumpkin (not pumpkin pie mix). Dogs love both!

Exercising the pudgy dog

There are two necessary steps to helping an overweight dog shed some pounds: feed fewer calories and burn more calories through exercise. Exercise is vital, but diving into a vigorous exercise program may be too taxing for an overweight dog. We want to safely work off the pounds, so slow and steady wins the race. In order to lose one pound, a dog must burn 3500 calories more than he consumes and this takes time. In general, the goal is to lose 1-2% of body weight every week.

Initially, two 15 minute trots may be too much to ask of the dog. The time and intensity of each exercise session depends on how much weight your dog has to lose and other factors in your dog's health as determined by your veterinarian. If your dog needs to lose 20% of his body weight you may start with intentional, non-stop walking. With walking, the energy (calories) used is proportionate to the distance traveled so if you are moving more slowly you may be able to go further to burn more calories.

Once your dog gets closer to his ideal weight you can increase the time and intensity of the workouts and as he builds muscle mass and endurance the pounds will come off more quickly. Until then, have patience. Dogs don't gain weight overnight and they won't lose it overnight either. And remember, exercise needs to continue after the weight is lost for your dog's healthy and happiness.

Example of a Journal Entry

Date	Feeding	Exercise	Weight	Changes/Notes
11/10/10	1/2 c am 1/2 c pm	20m am, 20m pm	33lbs	tired dog
11/11/10	1/2 c am 1/2 c pm	21m am, 20m pm	32.9	
11/12/10	1/2 c am 1/2 c pm	21m am, 21m pm	32.9	
11/13/10	1/3 c am 1/2 c pm	22m am, 21 m pm	32.6	
11/14/10	1/3 c am 1/2 c pm	22 m am, 20m pm	32.3	more endurance

What gets measured gets improved.

We all like to see the fruit of our labor. If we are going to put the effort in, we want to know that it is making a difference. It's difficult if not impossible to track the gradual improvement of the health of our dog if we don't measure and document our daily efforts. The best way to keep track is to maintain a journal in which you document how much you feed, how long you walk, weight, and any changes in the dog. Table 2 gives a sample of a possible journal entry tracking changes. However, if you are more electronically minded, there are online journals available, like diaryland. com, where you can track and measure improvements.

If you have a puppy or adolescent dog that doesn't have a weight problem, then it's your job to think about prevention. Don't wait for you dog to get overweight before you make a plan for health. Lean dogs live almost 2 years longer on average, so keep your pup lean.

CHAPTER EIGHT
Puppies are for Play

Your 8 month old puppy zips and zooms around the house and you wonder where he gets all of that energy? And more importantly, how can you calm him down?

Puppies, defined as any dog under a year old, need exercise, too. The key to exercising a puppy is to keep it short, keep it fun, and keep it low intensity and low impact. According to Dr. Steven B. Fox, a dog's growth plates of the bones do not close until a dog reaches 14 months old. Also, just like human children puppies often aren't very coordinated and they have undeveloped muscles. He recommends that any type of serious conditioning program should be delayed until 14 months of age to prevent injury. Still, there are lots of fun things you can do with your puppy that will calm him down and help him grow up into a strong calm adult.

Very young puppies just don't have the concentration skills, coordination or endurance to do much more than play freely. You can attempt some basic obedience skills with your young puppy and get him acclimated to a leash and collar. Once your vet approves, you can begin introducing your puppy to new places, new people and, of course, other puppies to play with. But dogs this age should not be taken on deliberate walks or jogs or asked to perform any type of strength training. Since proprioception exercises are not physically challenging you can attempt to get your puppy to do the ladder exercise as long as you keep your expectations low. If the puppy is too small for the ladder, try asking him to walk across a plank laid flat on the ground to build his skills.

Older puppies, 6 months +, are starting to grow into their bodies and build a little bit of strength and endurance. They should be mature enough to nail down the basic obedience commands: sit, down, come, stay, and walk nicely on a leash. This is a great time to take your dog to the park (on or off leash) to practice obedience commands under distraction. If your dog has some dog playmates, try setting up play dates for your him to enjoy the company of other dogs and start learning doggy-manners. You can and should continue to do some proprioception work with your dog at this age to improve his coordination and balance. Older pups have likely matured enough to enjoy playing strength training games with you like chase and a little bit of tug or water fetch which will also help them burn off some puppy energy. Asking your dog to run a few hills is also a great energy burner and back end muscle builder. However, older puppies are still not strong or developed enough to do endurance work, so continue to wait to under later to introduce long leash jogs.

Once a dog hits 14 months old you can slowly start to do intentional leash walks and jogs. However, a 14 month old dog does not have much muscle mass, so the ramp up time from 15 minutes to a full 30 minute non-stop trot should be extended over a few months and only performed 3 or 4 times a week until the dog has acclimated. A dog this age is very energetic though so he should be given plenty of opportunity to run and play freely with you and with other dogs. Two words: Dog Park. It is also now safe to initiate a strength-training program and you may do an unlimited amount of proprioception work. Don't forget to play with your puppy!

CHAPTER NINE

It is Never too Late...

The motto for a senior dog is "Just keep moving."
It is never too late to start a healthy habit.

Old age is not a disease but an ongoing process. Just
like humans, as dogs age they tend to slow down. Cells
don't function as efficiently so we don't generate as much
energy. We get injured more easily and repair injuries
more slowly. We tend to lose muscle mass as we age
and so our metabolism slows down. It's easier to gain
weight as we age. This means that our lean muscle to fat

ratio can easily get skewed. Muscle mass correlates with strength, balance, and coordination. Decrease in bone density. But this is not a reason to give up or give in.

There are "young" seniors and then there are geriatric seniors. Large breeds are considered geriatric around age 9, medium and smaller around age 11. Of course, the older the dog the slower and more gradual you must be in introducing new activities. It is vital that your senior dog is deemed healthy enough to start an exercise program by your veterinarian before you begin.

If your young senior or geriatric dog is having mobility problems, having trouble getting up from his nap or getting up the stairs, or your veterinarian has diagnosed him with joint disease like osteoarthritis, you may chose to find a rehabilitation clinic near you. Your dog is likely to improve joint health, increase range of motion, build muscle strength and reduce pain over the course of just a few rehab sessions. See Chapter Ten, When Injuries Happen, for information on finding and selecting an orthopedic and rehabilitation veterinarian.

Walking Always Works

The key elements with a senior dog is to keep his weight low and to keep him moving. Start with controlled low impact exercises like non-stop leash walks (not trots, yet.) With a walking gait, the energy used and number of calories burned is proportionate to the distance traveled. Distance is more important that speed, at least initially. So go slow and go long. Try to stay on soft surfaces like grass, dirt, sand, mulch or trails to absorb impact on the joints.

Watch how the dog responds to exercise: is he stiff or sore? Is he excited about going? If he does well, go further. If joint pain or stiffness increases after exercise, cut the time of the walk in half and go more often. Instead of one 30 minute walk you may want to cut back to 3 x 10 minute walking sessions and ramp up from there. Remember, to either increase duration or speed at a time in a workout, but not both.

Uphill

Speaking of ramps, walking up inclines is excellent exercise for a senior dog! A dog naturally leans forward into movement. When a dog walks his front arms and shoulders carry more of his body weight than his back legs. For long bodied dogs like Dachshunds, the front arms carry as much as 80% of the dogs weight!

A dog's arms can get plenty of exercise with

just normal daily life but the back end doesn't get enough exercise; this explains why senior dogs tend to have atrophied muscles in their lower backs, hips and legs. However, when a dog walks uphill his body weight is forced backwards making his hips and legs work harder. You will likely extend the life of your senior dog by simply making him walk hills and ramps.

Swimming

Walking isn't the only exercise you can try out with your golden-age dog. Swimming is often a welcomed addition to a walking or trotting program. A senior dog that enjoys swimming will be happy to do a few water fetches. Or, you may want to put a halter on your dog, connect him to a leash and then you both wade out to deeper water. You hold the leash and let him swim in place, starting with 5 minutes and gradually adding time.

Your senior dog would also benefit from playing a few games, some gentle stretches and he could even perform a few repetitions of the strength builders. If nothing else, you should teach your dog the Sitting

Pretty exercise. Any dog can learn this trick and it is a fantastic workout for the core muscles. Just ask your dog to sit and then wave some tempting treat above his head as a lure to get him to raise up to grab it. It may take a senior 10 days or more to build the muscle strength to actually "beg" but keep at it!

Now more than ever it is important to keep a journal so that you and your vet can track how your dog is responding to his new activities and change up his routine on occasion to address the areas where 'father time' is chipping away.

Sample journal for a Senior dog

Date	Food	Meds	Weight	Changes/Notes
11/10/10	1/2 c am 1/2 c pm	20m am, 20m pm	22lb	Loved it!
11/11/10				
11/12/10				
11/13/10				
11/14/10				

At this stage of life, your senior dog will appreciate the relaxation and stress relief gained from the endorphins released during his exercise... especially if he tends to get a little grumpy. He will also really appreciate the time he gets to spend with you every day.

Rest is very important for an older dog. Your senior should always get one full day off from exercise every vweek to sleep and lie around the house. Learn to recognize signs when your dog needs to recuperate.

CHAPTER TEN
Get your Dog off the Dole

Dogs like to work. We all may enjoy a few days of just lazing around the house but after a while it get old. This is true for our dogs, too. In the last twenty years or so, people have created hundreds of ways that we can put our dogs back to work – no, they may not bring in a paycheck (though some do!) but they do have a purpose in life.

Your dog's first task in his Daytimer, of course, is to go running with you. But there is so much more your dog can do. Any dog can be taught to do some

practical retrieving – your trainer can show you how to teach your dog to get the newspaper, find your keys or the TV remote. Dogs can be taught to close cabinet doors or turn off the light switch or put your kid's toys back into the toy box. If you are creative you can teach your dog to do just about anything.

Backpacking

Most medium and large dogs love to carry backpacks. If you have a sporting or working breed and your dog needs to work a little harder on your daily runs you can get him to wear a backpack. Running with a pack is an excellent endurance and strength training exercise.

A dog backpack is a handy piece of equipment. In the summer he can carry water for you both to drink. He can carry his own poop bags. He can carry snacks or part of a picnic for your family. And if you are a hiker or backpacker, he can be trained and conditioned to carry his own gear. If he is a big dog like a St. Bernard he can probably carry some of your gear too.

There are two tips to successful and safe backpacking with your dog: proper fit and proper conditioning for weight. The backpack should fit squarely over his shoulders, NOT on his back. When you shop for a backpack be sure to try it on your dog to ensure that the straps can be comfortably adjusted so that the pack doesn't sit on the dog's back.

It is important that your dog is properly and slowly conditioned to carry weight in his backpack. The rule of thumb for most dogs is to carry no more than 20% of his body weight (breeds who were bred to carry heavy loads can carry 25%). After purchasing a backpack, you will want to get your dog used to the feel of wearing it so put it on him empty and let him wear it around for a while.

Once he doesn't notice the pack anymore you can start to add weight. Start with 10% of his body weight and evenly distribute it on both sides of the backpack. Let him wear the backpack on one of your daily jogs three days a week. For medium dogs you can add as much as ¼ of a pound every week and larger dogs can add ½ pound every week until he reaches they reach maximum weight. Be sure to evenly distribute the weight in both panniers of the pack.

This is a new physical challenge to your dog so keep an eye on him to see how he responds and track it in your journal. Since the dog is now carrying more than his body weight it is important to stick to running on soft surfaces.

Dog Sports

You may have seen a television program or a live demo of dogs doing fun activities like diving off docks, complicated retrievals and even running through obstacle courses. Welcome to the world of dog sports where humans and canines are a team!

Participation in dog sports is on the rise; there is a dog sport for every breed, cross-breed, size and age of dog. What makes these activities so popular is each one combines the benefits of physical training, the mental stim ulation of work and the fun and stress relief of play.

Sport	Description	Breeds
Agility	One of the most popular dog sports. In this sport dog run through an obstacle course and are judged on time and ability.	Open to all breeds. Most frequently seen in the ring: Papillons, Shetland Sheepdogs, Border Collies, Corgis, Australian Shepherds and Parson Russel Terriers
Field Trials and Hunt Tests	Dogs retrieve from long distances and with complex paths	Divided by Breed. Clubs are open to retrievers, spaniels, pointers and the hunting hounds, like Bassets and Beagles.
Herding Trials	Dogs get to herd cattle and are tested on their timing and instinct.	Open to Herding Breeds like Australian Shepherd, Cattle Dogs, Collies, Corgis, Schnauzers, Germans Shepherds, and Rotties
Earthdog Trials	Do you have a digger or a varmint killer? Dogs are tested on their ability to track small animals through underground burrows.	Terriers and Dachshunds

if you enjoy the idea of conditioning your dog, you enjoy competition and your dog is raring to go, dog sports may be for you.

The table above describes some of the more popular dog sports. Most of these sports are open to breeds of all types, but some breeds are more interested in and competitive in one sport over others. For a comprehensive review of all dog sporting options see www.workingdogweb.com.

Even if you aren't a competitive person, you can still enjoy participating in a dog sport at home and in your community. The most popular sport, agility, is easy to set up at home and perfect for any pet. There is lightweight agility equipment designed for backyard use available for purchase online. Dogs have a blast learning the obstacles.

CHAPTER ELEVEN

When Injuries Happen

Your dog sails off your back deck after a squirrel and trips over a root sticking out of the ground. As he runs back into the house you notice he's holding up a paw. In fact, he's not putting weight on his front left leg at all.

Uh oh. Now what?

Accidents happen. Even superbly trained highly conditioned professional athletes get injured. The most common injuries to dogs are muscle pulls, sprains and ligament injuries. But with today's advancements in veterinary medicine dogs are recovering from injuries quickly and easily and live happy active lives.

The first step immediately after an injury is to examine the dog. Is there a wound? If the dog is bleeding, apply direct pressure to the wound until the bleeding has slowed or stopped.

Then examine the leg for orthopedic problems:

- Move the toes: Are they painful?
- Broken? Are the paw pads cut?
- Flex and extend the leg: Does it feel broken? How does the dog respond?
- Look for swelling around a potential injury.

The next step is to rest the dog, preferably keep the dog quiet in a crate except for short on leash potty breaks. You can also apply an ice pack or cold compress to the injury for 10 minutes 4-5 times a day for the first few days. If the dog doesn't improve after 2 –3 days of rest and ice then it is time to see the vet. Please do not medicate the dog yourself. Consult your veterinarian before you give your dog any medication.

Sometimes a trip to the emergency vet is in order. If your dog shows the following signs do not hesitate to get your dog to the vet: an obvious break; non weight bearing in a limb and vocally painful: bleeding profusely: vomiting, fever or excessive lethargy after an injury.

An injury or an orthopedic problem is not the end of the world for your dog. Medical miracles are being performed every day in cutting edge veterinary rehabilitation clinics. They specialize in getting dogs back to running and playing – even dogs who have suffered from breaks, sprains, strains, ligament tears, dysplasia, arthritis, and spinal problems. Often, a dog graduates from rehabilitation in better physical condition than before his injury surfaced.

Veterinary Physical Rehabilitation

Rehabilitation is a fascinating new field of veterinary medicine. Some of the facilities rival what you would see in a professional sports team's gym complete with jetted hot tubs. Whether a dog's injury require surgery or not, the benefits of physical rehabilitation are evident: ease pain and speed recovery, improve flexibility and coordination, correct faulty bio-mechanics, and build muscle and endurance which helps prevent future injuries.

Rehab veterinarians use a wide variety of new modalities for treatment, and most rehab veterinarians prefer to start with the most holistic and least invasive treatments first. Here's just a short list of some tools used in veterinary rehab medicine:

- non-ablative lasers
- therapeutic ultrasound
- electric muscle stimulation
- massage therapy
- hydrotherapy
- trans-cutaneous electrical
- neuromuscular stimulation

The two most widely used methods of treatment are the underwater treadmill and the land or dry treadmill. Almost all dogs begin rehab on the underwater treadmill. Dogs that otherwise can't exercise due to their injury can often handle session in the underwater treadmill within days of being injured or after surgery. It is important to get the dog up and moving quickly to keep his circulation healthy, his muscles from atrophying, and of course, to keeps his spirits lifted.

The underwater treadmill is exactly what it sounds like – a treadmill that floods with water. Water has certain properties that make it useful for therapy. For the dog's comfort, the water is generally heated to improve flexibility, circulation and to ease sore muscles and joints. The buoyancy property of water diminishes the effect of gravity thus reducing the impact and stress on the body. It also helps with balance and will keep a dog vertical. The higher the water levels the higher the degree of buoyancy and the lower the degree of weight bearing during exercise.

Dogs with an injured a limb that are reluctant to use it will often start using the limb again in the water due to the buoyancy. It may hurt a 30 pound dog to bear full weight on an injured limb, but he may feel comfortable bearing 38%, or 11 pounds, of weight. Gradually the water level is lowered from shoulder to elbow to wrist as the dog's injury heals and he shows improved function and mobility.

Have you ever tried walking through thigh high water? It's a real workout! Water provides a lot of resistance. As the water levels are lowered and buoyancy is reduced the level of resistance increases which builds muscle mass. Once the dog has mastered the underwater treadmill he graduates to workouts on the land treadmill until he regains strength, balance and endurance.

The cost and length of treatment at a rehabilitation clinic is dependent on the severity of the injury and what the goals of treatment are. Some dogs go through several weeks of inpatient treatment where the dog lives at the clinic. Other dogs with less extensive injuries attend the clinic for treatment 3 times a week for several weeks.

Owners of obese dogs often use the services of a rehabilitation clinic to assist with weight loss and senior or arthritic dogs also benefit from rehab to loosen stiff joints and muscles and manage pain. Most dog graduates of rehabilitation clinics return to the clinic 2-3 times a year for check ups and to have their exercise programs adjusted to build the dogs weaker areas or to manage the areas where father-time is chipping away.

To find a veterinary rehabilitation clinic with an excellent record you will need to do a little homework. Ask local surgeons whom they would recommend. Ask the clinic for references from dog owner clients. Ask for a tour of the facility. Perhaps the best resource is people who compete with their dogs in agility or field trials. Many of these people have a lot of time, training and money staked on the dog's performance so if the dog is injured they seek out the best of the best. You can call your local agility or field trial clubs and ask if they can direct you to an excellent facility.

CHAPTER TWELVE

Go out into the World

Hank's Story

Hank is a beautiful 11 month old 60 pound Lab mix puppy. His owners called me because they feared that their dog was aggressive and he was all but impossible to walk because he was such a strong leash puller. When I first met Hank at the door he jumped all over me in excitement and when I tried to take him for a walk he almost pulled my shoulder out of socket. He was a strong energetic puppy! He would lunge after anything that moved and he pulled even harder if he spotted another dog. I asked Hank's owners about how much exercise he gets and about how much time he gets to spend socializing and playing with other dogs. Hank mostly was turned out into the backyard to run around for exercise and because he was so difficult to walk he didn't get taken out to experience new things very often.

Hank was a big furry bundle of pent up puppy energy! All that pent up energy was the reason behind the jumping and pulling and over the top exuberance that the owners mistook for aggression. We decided to take Hank to the off-leash park to introduce him to other dogs and safely let him run to his hearts content. It took Hank all of 20 seconds to decide that he LOVED the dog park. He was thrilled to be off leash running around with other dogs and burning off his energy. With teary eyes, Hank's owners watched their dog having such a great time and committed to bringing him to play at least three times a week.

I saw Hank three weeks later. This time he calmly met me at the door with all four paws on the ground. His owners reported that his leash pulling had all but vanished so that they could start walking him regularly again. Hank was a different dog, the calm centered dog he was born to be, because of his new exercise routine and social time at the dog park.

As important as exercise is to a calm, well-centered dog,

so is socialization. A well socialized dog gets along with other dogs, children, adults, elderly people, adapts to new surroundings, and is comfortable with change. A poorly socialized dog acts fearful (barking, cowering, nipping) in new situations. They pull and/or bark excitedly whenever they see another dog. An under socialized dog can be people aggressive, dog aggressive, reacts negatively to children, wheelchairs, floppy hats, flapping raincoats, rats, etc. A dog that isn't properly socialized will never be able to enjoy their life to the fullest. Having a non-socialized dog also means limiting the extent of where and when you can be with your pet.

Dogs are by nature social and curious animals which is why they make such great companions for us. It is important for dogs of all ages to get out into the world and experience new things, learn to accept new situations and most importantly, learn that you will keep them safe in all situations.

The term "socialization" is used a lot in dog training, but the concept is not complex. It has only 2 parts: introducing the dog to new things (people, dogs, places, sounds, smells, sights, etc) and building an ironclad trust with your dog so that he feels safe in new situations. If a dog is properly socialized he is more likely to be a calm, happy and non-fearful member of your family. Socialization is not just the work of puppies though. On-going socialization with an adult dog is key to giving him proper mental stimulation and will help him not grow stale.

Socialize

The beginning of socialization starts with you, the owner. As soon as you meet your new dog your first and most important task is to build a rock solid relationship of trust with him. As you get to know your dog, and he you, you will learn who he is, what he likes and dislikes and what really gets him turned on. You then can start working on becoming the most exciting and amazing thing in your dog's life – more exciting than food, more exciting than squirrels, even more exciting than the UPS truck. The keys to magnetizing your dog to you is satisfying his needs to run, play and work.

You get to set the stage for the dog's life and his experiences in your home. From day one he will watch you and start setting his core beliefs, so to speak, about how life is: is life chaotic? Or is life orderly, consistent and reliable? Is life scary? Are people scary? Or are people safe and fun? Do children chase, frighten and antagonize me? Do I have to protect myself from them? Or are children calm quiet sources of enjoyable touches and treats? Will other dogs hurt me? Or are they fun playmates?

Every dog, like every person, has his own temperament and personality. Some are shy and some are confident. Some are people-oriented and some are more family-only dogs. Some dogs enjoy rough and tumble play and some dogs prefer a more quiet and controlled play time. There is no wrong or bad personality type – your dog is who he is. But socialization can soften a dog's personality extremes. While he may never ask for belly rubs from a stranger, a shy dog can learn that attention from a new person is safe and

tolerable. An overly outgoing dog can learn that not every person or every dog wants to be the object of his exuberance. It is important to emphasize that introductions to new things, especially with puppies, should be slow and deliberate and with lots of food. If your dog shows signs of fear (barking, growling, shaking, shrinking back, or if he has a look of emotional collapse in his eyes) you need to immediately remove your dog from the situation and start more slowly next time and move more gradually. You want to make sure that every experience your puppy has is a positive experience.

You must remember to think like a dog and feel like a dog: just because you think something is good and fun doesn't mean the dog does. You may think that that your puppy feels safe if he is in his crate watching while the kids act like kids, yelling and running about. But the pup may feel threatened by the children's behavior. It is your job to keep your dog feeling safe and calm, not fearful or frenzied.

Maturity plays a huge role in how much you expose your dog to. Puppies are babies and babies can easily be over stimulated by their environments. Just being allowed to roam around your house while the kids are playing and the television is on could over stimulate a pup. Habitually an over-stimulated puppy can grow into a nervous high-strung dog. It is important that puppies are given plenty of time to sleep in a quiet calm area of the house to recoup and unwind, both physically and emotionally. Again, you must be the expert on your pup (and adult dog). Signs of fear or frenzy cannot be ignored.

If your puppy tends to be high-strung or sensitive, you may want to help him stay calm by keeping most of his first interactions and introductions to strange new things and new people outside of your house. As much as we love to have our dogs indoors with us – and they love it too – the outdoors is their natural habitat. Nature has a calming and unwinding effect on dogs. Imagine if you drop a metal pot on the floor of your kitchen – it would make huge reverberating noise. Now imagine you drop that same pot on your concrete porch outside. It doesn't make that much noise, does it? The outdoors has the same effect on a dog – what is too much indoors can be

tolerable outdoors. You can relieve some of the pressures of early socialization by keeping the activities outside.

Dog parks

Off leash dog parks are a wonderful way to get your dog out into the world. Most parks are fenced off or in a remote area, so they are a safe place to play and train with your dog. Of course, dogs need and enjoy the company of other dogs. At the dog park, your dog can be a dog – sniff things, pee on things, run wild, play chase and wrestle and learn good dog manners from other dogs. Dog parks are also full of dog friendly people – people who would love to meet your dog. So, it is a great place to help your dog make new human friends.

How and when you use your local dog park depends on your dog's personality and what types of dogs and people frequent your park. If you have a big confident and outgoing dog like Hank, you can probably just open the gate and let him go without worrying about how well he will acclimate. Most dogs can get their bearings within the first few minutes and will have fun.

If you have a shy sensitive dog, or a dog who hasn't spent much time with other dogs you will want to be watchful of your dog and take steps to make sure that he feels safe and is having a good time. If your dog is apprehensive as you approach the gate, you may want to spend your first visit playing with him and treating him outside the fence where the dog feels safe. Then perhaps visit the park a few times without the dog and see when it is quiet or when you're dog can be there alone to check it out and get used to the environment.

It is very important that puppies get to spend time with other dogs where they can learn dog skills, like how to play fair and other dog etiquette. The dog park may be a good resource for you. Before you take your puppy or shy dog to the dog park you may want to go there by yourself to check it out: are the dogs friendly? Do they play nicely with each other? Are there any boisterous dogs to watch out for? Are the owners responsible and paying attention to what the dogs are up to? Just as you use caution about the friends your kids have you will want to use caution about the dogs your puppy spends time with.

There are a few things you can do to help your dog settle in at an off-leash park during his first few visits. Remember that you want to be intentional about how you introduce your dog to new things. The dogs already playing in the park will probably rush over to the gate to checkout the new arrival. Once you are inside the gate take off your dog's leash and keep walking! This is not the time to stop and meet the other dogs or introduce yourself to the humans – keep on walking around the park and your dog will follow you around.

After you and your pup have checked out the park continue to interact with your dog. Play chase. Play fetch. Practice commands. Don't ignore him. Watch how your dog interacts with other dogs. Let him sniff and be sniffed. If he shows an interest in joining in a game of doggy chase and wrestle, let him! The minute that he stops playing or looks tired or bored, leave. And of course, if you see the equivalent of a playground brawl brewing among the other dogs, call your dog to you and leave. Keep your first visit to the park relatively short and fun.

Puppies and young dogs (dogs under 2 years old) are malleable and easily influenced. They make sweeping generalization from each life experience. For example, if an 8 year old dog is bullied or bitten by another dog he is likely to specify that unpleasant event to that time and that dog. On the other hand, a young dog who is bullied or bitten by another dog is likely to generalize that experience so that he starts to be on guard for bullies all the time and sees every dog as a danger to him. A traumatic event on a young dog can be healed but it often requires time and work with a trainer. What defines a trauma is dependent on your dog's age and personality.

What is traumatizing to a puppy or dog may be things that we would never recognize: an overly-friendly and overwhelming greeting by another dog, getting swarmed by dogs at the dog park gate, play with a person or dog that gets too rough, a person who unintentionally threatens the dog, a child who pulls the dog's tail or teases with food. If the problem isn't corrected and the trauma left untreated the dog may develop fear or fear aggression. So it is critical to watch your dog closely and intervene before another dog or a person upsets him. This is the same for every new life experience with your puppy (and your adult dog). You must be vigilant. You are responsible for protecting him and ensuring that he is safe, feels safe and has happy and fun experiences and interactions only. You want your dog to trust you.

If you determine that your dog park is not suitable for you and your dog you should invite specific dogs that share your dog's personality and play style to a doggy playgroup.

Dog friendly stores

Another great venue for socializing your dog is to take him to dog friendly stores. Your dog can experience new things like tile flooring, automatic sliding glass doors, grocery carts, and lots of noises and smells. Of course, there will also be people with children and dogs of all breeds on leash for him to interact with. Some of the stores even offer doggy social hours. Depending on your dog's personality and maturity, your first trip to the store could be fabulous or frightening. As always, monitor your dog's reactions and adjust your plan as needed.

When your dog gets comfortable with spending time in the store, if your local store is one of the large box stores, you can even go there during inclement weather to get in your 15-20 minute run by going up and down the aisles. The inherent distractions will be an excellent test of your dog's training and healing abilities.

The Car

Some of you are saying, "But my dog gets car sick!". Carsickness is frequently a behavioral issue rather than a medical problem. It's common for dogs to stop getting motion sick after starting a healthy exercise routine and play time. In the mean time, the you can socialize your dog to the car. Try feeding him his dinner in the parked car for a few days. Throw treats in the car for him to retrieve. Take very very very short drives with the windows open. Gradually, your dog will learn to love the car. And then you can take him every where you go.

CHAPTER THIRTEEN
When it's Time to Call Me, the Pro

Suppose you've followed these guidelines for exercise and play for a few months but your dog still wants to chase the UPS truck or snaps at your children. Your dog seems to be happier and more physically fit but something is still missing; there is something that isn't right or you feel a chink in your relationship with your dog and you don't know how to solve it.

Trust your instincts.

Many of us today share our homes with adopted dogs. We didn't get to raise them from puppyhood and we might not know their history. Some of our dogs were treated badly by their original owners and some were neglected. But frequently people with good intentions but with bad information simply don't raise their puppy in a healthy way and unintentionally harm the dog's heart and soul. Let's face it, like some of our children, some of our dogs are born super-sensitive and there is nothing wrong with that. Regardless of our dogs' histories, sometimes they have wounded temperaments.

Temperament is defined as the behavioral reflection of the heart (emotional center) of the dog. Regular exercise and stress relieving play will help these dogs cope on a day to day basis and over the long run it may heal the dogs that aren't deeply hurt. But special care is sometimes needed to heal dogs with seriously wounded temperaments.

Some of the signs of a wounded temperament are:
- ceaseless barking for no reason
- "from out of nowhere" biting and snapping
- cowering and shaking
- obsessive compulsive behaviors
- rage and panic biting

These dogs aren't bad or mean. They are simply acting in ways that feel right and safe to them.

It is never too early, or too late, to ask for help from a professional. If you feel uncomfortable with something going on with your dog or clearly if you see that your dog feels uncomfortable seek professional advice. First rule out a medical problem by taking your dog to a trusted veterinarian. After ruling out medical issues, seek the help of dog professional who understand the nature of the dog and knows how to help heal his temperament.

Final Thoughts

Does your dog chew your shoes when you leave him for the day? Does he almost yank your arm off when you try to take him for a walk? Does he dig up your backyard? Does he bite inappropriately?

If you've read this far you know the solution. For your dog to be calm, healthy and happy you must meet his needs. Your dog needs to:

1. RUN every day
2. PLAY with you to burn off stress
3. BUILD A STRONG BODY to live a long life
4. BE WITH DOGS –they speak his language
5. SPEND TIME WITH YOU to build a good relationship

GET OUT AND EXPLORE THE WORLD

You now know how to
Wag that Tail in Your Dog!

Now go put on your running shoes and get started.

MICHAELS-PACK.COM

Having trained and shown dogs my whole life, I want to put my knowledge and experience (and passion) to work. My goal is to help you understand and communicate better with your dog. In order to do that, I've provided Michaels-pack.com; a state of the art website that helps you understand and communicate better with your dog.

I will provide helpful information on various topics such as nutrition, behavior issues, dog thoughts etc. Most importantly, all training that I do is based on positive reinforcement coupled with an holistic method, making it as easy and rewarding as possible for you, the owner, to bond and create that magical connection that occurs when you and your best friend are synced in as one.

ABOUT THE AUTHOR

I'm very fortunate in that most of my day is spent with dogs. I get to see all types and breeds. From balanced well-centered dogs to emotional basket cases. The more I interact with them, the more I'm amazed at how much they can tolerate from their human partners. For all of our vaunted intelligence, we can show such a lack of empathy and understanding for these magnificent creatures that it blows me away. When a dog constantly lunges and pulls to see another dog, it should be obvious that it needs to be with its own kind. It's only natural. For the vast majority of us, don't we live in communities surrounded by our own kind? Hello!! Arrange play dates for your dog so they can socialize with their own kind. Let him romp and jump and sniff rear ends and BE A DOG!!

Understanding dogs is a work in progress. Their behavior and reactions to events are based on their instincts and senses. The most common error we make is trying to attribute human characteristics to our dogs behavior. Dogs are not "spiteful". They don't think in those terms. I have seen many people who tell me their puppy went in the house "out of spite." Not true. In my opinion, dogs have a higher sense of order and value than that.

When a fenced-in dog starts barking at another dog as it walks by, it does not mean he is "vicious" or is looking to get out and attack the other dog. Most of the times, if the fenced-in dog ever did get out, he would probably go over to the other dog , exchange sniffs, and start playing. Barking is how dogs talk. In this case, the barking was simply communicating the frustration of being behind the fence.

Dogs are not suicide bombers. They do not automatically attack each and fight to the death once off the leash. Dogs have two methods of dealing with confrontation, fight or flight. While some will choose the latter, a vast majority of dogs would rather walk away from a fight given the opportunity. Dogs have been around for 25,000 years, give or take a century or two. It doesn't make sense that they would innately seek out their own species and try to annihilate one another.

"It's all about understanding and communication."
- Michael Schaier: CPDT-K.A., ABC-D.T., AKC-C.G.C. Evaluator

RESOURCES

acsma.org – American Canine Sports Medicine Association

Caninesports.com – List of dog sports and how to get involved.

diaryland.com – an online diary that makes record keeping easy

DogRunDog.com – national database of dog friendly races

Dogscooter.com – teach your dog to pull you on wheels, a wheelchair, or a scooter.

Fitfordog.com – dog blogs, ideas on dog workouts

michaels-pack.com – where you find me, Michael

Rehabvets.org – American Association of Rehab Vets

sarahallison.com – where you find my designer, Sarah

workingdogweb.com – list and description of dog sports

47344786R00080

Made in the USA
San Bernardino, CA
27 March 2017